LOVE OR LAWS?

Essays on Law, Policy and Psychiatry
Peter Fritz Walter

Codependence
Coping with Addiction, Sadism and Abuse

Eight Dynamic Patterns of Living
Base Elements of True Civilization

Emotional Flow
A Holistic Approach to Healing Sadism

Love or Laws?
When Law Punishes Life

Minotaur Unveiled
A Historical Assessment of Adult-Child Sexual Interaction

Natural Order
Thesis, Antithesis and Synthesis in Human Evolution

Pedophilia Revisited
The Making of a Crime for Justifying Lacking Social Policy

The Commercial Exploitation of Abuse
A Study on Social Policy

The Legal Split in Child Protection
Overcoming the Double Standard

The Roots of Violence
Why Humans Are Not by Nature Violent

LOVE OR LAWS?

When Law Punishes Life

Peter Fritz Walter

Published by Sirius-C Media Galaxy LLC

Business Filings Incorporated

108 West 13th St., Wilmington, DE 19801, USA

©2018 Peter Fritz Walter. Some rights reserved.

Essays on Law, Policy and Psychiatry, Vol. 4

Creative Commons Attribution 4.0 International License

This publication may be distributed, used for an adaptation or for derivative works, also for commercial purposes, as long as the rights of the author are attributed. The attribution must be given to the best of the user's ability with the information available. Third party licenses or copyright of quoted resources are untouched by this license and remain under their own license.

The moral right of the author has been asserted

Set in Avenir Light and Trajan Pro

Designed by Peter Fritz Walter

ISBN 978-1-983988-82-0

Publishing Categories
Law / Criminal Law / Juvenile Offenders

Publisher Contact Information
publisher@sirius-c-publishing.com
http://sirius-c-publishing.com

Author Contact Information
pfw@peterfritzwalter.com

About Dr. Peter Fritz Walter
http://peterfritzwalter.com

About the Author

Parallel to an international law career in Germany, Switzerland and the United States, Dr. Peter Fritz Walter (Pierre) focused upon fine art, cookery, astrology, musical performance, social sciences and humanities.

He started writing essays as an adolescent and received a high school award for creative writing and editorial work for the school magazine.

After finalizing his law diplomas, he graduated with an LL.M. in European Integration at Saarland University, Germany, in 1982, and with a Doctor of Law title from University of Geneva, Switzerland, in 1987.

He then took courses in psychology at the University of Geneva and interviewed a number of psychotherapists in Lausanne and Geneva, Switzerland. His interest was intensified through a hypnotherapy with an Ericksonian American hypnotherapist in Lausanne. This led him to the recovery and healing of his inner child.

After a second career as a corporate trainer and personal coach, Pierre retired in 2004 as a full-time writer, philosopher and consultant.

His nonfiction books emphasize a systemic, holistic, cross-cultural and interdisciplinary perspective, while his fiction works and short stories focus upon education, philosophy, perennial wisdom, and the poetic formulation of an integrative worldview.

Pierre is a German-French bilingual native speaker and writes English as his 4th language after German, Latin and French. He also reads source literature for his research works in Spanish, Italian, Portuguese, and Dutch. In addition, Pierre has notions of Thai, Khmer, Chinese, Japanese, and Vietnamese.

All of Pierre's books are hand-crafted and self-published, designed by the author. Pierre publishes via his Delaware company, Sirius-C Media Galaxy LLC, and under the imprints of IPUBLICA and SCM (Sirius-C Media).

Dedicated to the late Dr. Edward Brongersma, Lawyer and Senator of the Dutch Senate (1911-1998) who was a long-term trustworthy friend and intellectually inspiring pen pal for more than twenty years.

The author's profits from this book are being donated to charity.

Contents

Introduction   9
What are Sex Laws Good For?

Chapter One   21
Childlove and Sensuality

Chapter Two   29
Childlove and Normalcy

Chapter Three   37
When Law Punishes Life

Statutory Rape   45
Child Molestation and Abuse   50
Law Reform   54
Love Reform   63

Bibliography   69
Contextual Bibliography

Personal Notes   89

Introduction

What are Sex Laws Good For?

What are sex laws good for? Are they regulating sexual behavior? Are they helping the state supervise what we do in bed, and with whom? Are they protecting minors?

Or are they safeguarding morality?

What is the reason they have been established in the first place, and when? And by whom? Are they built upon rational and verifiable principles, or upon irrational assumptions, or the dubious term 'public morals,' which ghosts around in legal textbooks.

What about facets that show the complexity of non-sadistic childlove, and its closeness to caring, loving behavior that is typical for the parent-child relation? The definition of the paraphilias contain that element of potential harm, of dangerousness, and also the clause of lacking consent.

American sexologist Dr. Moser writes that this definition is flawed, as it can be shown that *even sexual sadists* choose their partners according to their need for consenting relationships; newer research showed in addition that they do find their partners, as there are many more people consenting to this kind of unusual sex interaction that involves bondage, sharp objects, and here, well a certain dangerousness of it all. But it's not true that sexual sadists were rapists in that they needed to have non-consenting intercourse. Dr. Moser made that very clear in his paper.

> —Charles Allan Moser, DSM-IV-TR and the Paraphilias: an argument for removal, with Peggy J. Kleinplatz, Journal of Psychology and Human Sexuality 17 (3/4), 91-109 (2005).

However, he makes a clear distinction regarding adult-child sexual relations, not from the psychiatric point of view, but because of criminal law. Laws can only be changed by the lawmaker and we need to respect what is set in place. The present study makes no exception here, and I can only say in full agreement with Dr. Moser that what I can do here is to show there are arguments that a future lawmaker may decide differently on the question.

INTRODUCTION

I am going to show in this essay the interesting *parallels between childlove and sensuality*, the importance of sensuality especially for children and adolescents, and their often unfulfilled need for more sensuality. Hence, when the pedophile relation remains in the realm of the sensual, without stepping into the outright sexual, then not only do criminal laws not apply, but also from a social and ethical point of view, there is virtually nothing that can reasonably be forwarded against such kind of relations, as the behavior on the side of the adult is simply caring, not demanding, and not offending.

Besides, I also describe behaviors that well fall under criminal law, but I describe them to show their sensual and non-paraphilic character. I assume that children do have the ability to consent to pleasures given and taken. I also put up a hypothesis, namely that it's possible that a number of those who call themselves 'pedophiles' do not actually search out sex with children, but tender *sensual* relations that have a predominantly caring character. While in their fantasies, they may well desire penetration, they somehow manage to hold back because of the obvious *vulnerability* of the child partner, to even

attempt it. Hence, an argument could be made to treat non-penetrative adult-child sexual relations differently than penetrative ones.

Further, I am going to elucidate the question if pedophilia is considered as 'criminal behavior' simply because of the fact it's regarded as abnormal? Hence, we have to ask, is there any 'normal' sexual behavior; in other words, can a standard of sexual normalcy be defined at all?

After, these preliminary questions, I come to the essential, namely the strangest body of law there is in the world, *sex laws*.

In my career as a lawyer I have dealt with these laws quite a bit, as they were my particular research topic, while I was not the only jurist to be disgusted by them. I remember that in our criminal law class at *Saarland University* law faculty, Professor Dr. Krause, criminologist, was long before me! He said that none of our so-called sex laws had merited the qualifier 'law' as they were for the most part arbitrary injunctions, built upon extra-legal considerations, such as *moral opinions,* instead of being drafted as *rational and verifiable deeds*. In addition, he showed us with many examples that most of these laws are

INTRODUCTION

flagrant violations of constitutional guarantees, especially the guarantee of *nulla poena sine lege*, also known as *due process*, and thus of the very foundations of democracy.

After a year of postgraduate research conducted in the United States, at the *University of Georgia Law School*, I was so revolted by the disturbing current sex laws that I put myself at work to draft a legal bill that intently liberates all forms of mutually consenting sexual behavior from state supervision and control and leaves the stress solely upon cases involving physical and sexual violence. In this draft bill, that I am going to publish and discuss further down, I propose a law that does not punish love or life, but only violence which is something no responsible society should tolerate.

In my attempt to publish that first paper on physical and sexual violence against children, I was rejected by three publishers, one from Germany, one from the Netherlands and one from the United States. My paper was found to be either 'too feminist' or 'too revolting,' depending on the orientation of the publisher. But I was encouraged to persist in my efforts, for example by Françoise Dolto (1908-1988),

the late French child therapist and author of worldwide renown that I knew in person. Dr. Dolto agreed with me that sex laws as they are at present, and especially the laws for the protection of minors, with their legal consent ages, are really punishing life, and that their effect upon minors is all but protective; she found that these laws namely enslave children and rob them of their body.

On the other hand, it has to be seen that many psychoanalysts, and especially those, like Dolto, who follow the Freudian approach, are double-tongued in that on one hand they concede the child the right for self gratification in form of masturbation, but on the other deny the child real erotic relationships with a mate, and thus *partner relations.*

In fact, from the moment Freud rejected Reich's activism for children having erotic peer relations, with the argument that culture has to prevail, psychoanalysis by and large backed up Western society's persistent denial of children's free love life.

Sex laws seldom hit their goal because few people are inclined to follow legal rules that are off-track, irrational, ineffective, unjust or arbitrary. This is true for whatever legislation, not only for sex laws, but equally

INTRODUCTION

for alcohol or drug prohibitions. There appears to be a paradox: prohibitions contain an *inherent seduction to be broken*, even if there is draconic punishment waiting for the law breaker.

Democracy can be measured on the scale of its prohibitory statutes. A system that regards its members as irresponsible wheels in a machine will tend to rule all and everything about them, leaving them little personal choice, and granting them only a *minimum amount of personal freedom*. Such a system will try to impose strict inflexible rules of conduct upon each individual and leave it to the judiciary to deal with those who offend the ant republic.

Anglo-Saxon terminology is in this respect revealing in that it speaks of the *offender* and the *sex offender*. These terms show that under the present paradigm criminal law actually retaliates against people who *offend the system* and that victim protection is a fake concern. Thus, we are still in the midst of the Middle-Ages. Furthermore, the term *sex offender* is outright ridiculous whatever one understands under it; nobody can offend sex, and sex cannot offend the system. So who does offend what in this truly criminal legal terminology? The so-called

offender then is actually not a sex offender but rather a 'morality offender.'

By contrast, a society that basically trusts its individuals, and regards them as *responsible citizens* will formulate its criminal laws *only as a regulatory means for extreme, violent or extremely dangerous behavior.* In other words, such a society will only be inclined to use criminal laws for the purposes of confronting violent and thus non-consenting sexual behavior. Since violence is violence *regardless of the form it takes*, the democratic society envisioned by this bill will consider love and sexuality as basic forms of human expression and togetherness. It will apply restrictions only where *violence is superimposed upon sex or linked to sex* in a way that sex becomes a weapon to overpower, to subdue or to humiliate the sexual partner. Thus, the target behavior for criminal laws will be *violence*, and not sex. In other words, it is the element of *violence* that will qualify for sexual behavior being illegal.

From the moment we liberalize sexuality from its moralistic stigma, in much the same way as we have done for homosexuality, and children from child protection, which are both residues of inquisitory

INTRODUCTION

church laws and, as such, have no place in a modern legal system, we have no choice but admit that *sexuality, for people of whatever age, cannot reasonably be subjected to governmental regulation and interference.*

Regarding laws of consent, they have hardly any justification in a democratic society because their rationale is not really protection but rather paternalistic control and enslavement. What I am trying to say is that the current age of consent laws are a form of 'false imprisonment,' if you will, in the sense that the lives of children are heavily guarded and thus their very freedom is limited.

In addition, it has to be seen that sex laws are *largely ineffective to prevent sexual violence,* which is a fact everyone knows who reads the daily news.

On the other hand, there is no rationale to incriminate consenting love and sex between generations whatever the age of the partners may be. If sex laws at all protect anything, it's *morality*—or what in legal textbooks is called 'public morals,' which is a chewing-gum clause that can be used to put behind bars all and everybody when their opinions do not please the current government.

It's really a clause that opens the door to fascism and tyranny; while such clauses have been banned throughout our modern legal system, they still do their devil's business in sex laws.

You can justify practically all with such lofty expressions and it's precisely because of their lacking contours, that this term and many other similar terms are not fit for being part of modern criminal law as they violate constitutional liberties and are thus *unconstitutional*.

What I am saying is that if only one person would fight it through our legal system until the Supreme Court of the United States, there is a high probability that the catch-all clause of 'public morals' would be declared unconstitutional under the Constitution of the United States of America.

Karl Marx has convincingly shown that moral opinions in any given culture are but an overlay pattern or *roof structure* over the base structure that is made up by the social and economic conditions. You can also say the moralistic roof structure of any given society follows the economic root structure. This can exemplarily be shown with age-of-consent laws.

INTRODUCTION

With growing industrialization, and the corresponding longer educational cycle, the child remained a child for a more extended period of time. Still within the craftsmanship-subsistence culture of the Middle-Ages, social maturity of the child generally coincided with sexual maturity, at age twelve to fourteen.

Before the shift from liberalism to fascism in the years 1996-1998 in most Western countries, the reform of age-of-consent laws was seriously discussed by various national parliaments, such as for example the Italian, the German and the Dutch parliaments. In Germany, the *Green Party* came up with the proposal to lower the age of consent to 14 years of age.

In Holland, the situation was even more liberal as the police did not persecute sua sponte any contravention to the age of consent, when the child was more than 12 years old. Only in case that both parents and child submitted a written demand for criminal persecution, the police enforced the law.

Another point of discussion were homosexual pedosexual contacts; it was said that they should eventually be treated in the same way as heterosexual pedosexual contacts. Traditionally, even in Holland,

these relations were treated differently. And in most States of the United States, they are treated differently as well. For example in Georgia, the age of consent for girls is eighteen, for boys twenty-one.

As there is no rational basis for the discrimination of same-sex pedoerotic contacts, most parliamentary committees wanted to abolish them, as they had been abolished in Holland after the spectacular intervention of Senator Dr. Edward Brongersma who was charged with a six-months prison sentence for having had sex with a boy of sixteen years of age.

However, Dr. Brongersma fought against the judgment and eventually won the legal action against the Dutch Government, and as a result the penal code was changed to abolish any difference between heterosexual and homosexual adult-child sexual relations.

It is obvious that the lowering of ages of consent cannot qualify for a real paradigm change! This kind of liberalization rests with the old repressive patriarchal paradigm. And when we look behind the curtain, we understand that the only purpose of this so-called reform was political day-time fuss, and not a real change of basic beliefs.

Chapter One

Childlove and Sensuality

Children whose access to natural sensuality has been barred are at the onset of neurosis, of psychosis, of schizophrenia.

The repression of sensuality is a crime against the child, against the new generations, against humanity! Sensuality is inextricably linked with awareness, with sensitiveness. It's a form of acute awareness of the present moment, a peculiar state of lucidity!

To repress sensuality means to lower awareness to a lesser-than-human level, a level of evolution that is far lower than the animal level.

Some of the more visible results of this emosexual mutilation is Cartesian reasoning, scientism, reductionism and intellectualism. And as Michel Odent pertinently coined it, another undesirable

effect of this phenomenon is what he called the 'scientification of love.'

—Michel Odent, The Scientification of Love (1999).

Emotional intelligence is not possible without sensuality, body care, and a high amount of freedom for play. Every culture that represses sensuality and makes religious perversion its main paradigm creates violence and reduces happiness on earth. In these cultures, that are now unfortunately the reigning and most powerful nations on the globe, the free body play of children is manipulated in the most shameful way. The attention of the child is intently directed away from the body and toward toys that in some way replace the body. Pleasure is channeled into lifeless objects and taken away from its source that is the body, whereby the body is betrayed from early life. This cultural betrayal of the body is a sin against life and brings about deadly disease, mental illness, genetic degeneration and premature aging.

The specific sensual pleasure in childlove does not contain plastic nor artificial flavors or pesticides. It's a remembrance of one's own body play years ago, and this both for the adult and the child. *Thus, it simply is*

natural. There are other stimuli that can be observed and extracted from a multitude of individual reports.

For the adult, what contributes to sensual arousal for a child is the smallness of the child and their limbs, for the child it's, in analogy the tallness of the adult and their limbs.

The specific arousal value for a man when having sex with a child or when fantasizing about sex with a child is related to the smaller size of the child, their agile movements, their more flexible limbs, their higher skin tonus, their spontaneity, their fresh natural smell, their sometimes fish-like graciousness when they get excited and roll under the hands of their lover, their beautiful hair, and so forth, combined with a certain clumsiness that comes from the fact that they still have to learn the love game.

Other sensual pleasures typically are related to the innocent carefreeness of children and the fact that their consciousness is acute when doing body play and not distracted by smoking or drinking habits, that, as we all know, considerably lower our level of awareness. Thus, the intensity of sensual touch with a child is per se greater along these lines than with an adult.

To give a voice to the contrary view, let me again reference Bronislaw Malinowski's research with the Trobriand culture. The Trobriands, a tribal culture in New Guinea, who are sexually permissive with their children, believe that pedophilia is the result of a lack of sexual maturity. They laugh when, what rarely happens in their culture, a man shows sexual interest in children. They are permissive toward childlove, but cannot understand why somebody could possibly be interested in a creature that is not experienced in sex and also physically not really in state to perform all possible forms of copulation. Thus childlovers, in this culture, are not threatened, not despised and not discarded—they are ridiculed by the whole village! People just laugh at them as they cannot understand how somebody could be requiring so little from a sexual partner.

And behold, some firmly heterosexual men I have interviewed about childlove told me they co not feel aggression or hate toward pedophiles but cannot help smiling about them since they can't understand why they did not prefer a young and experienced woman over a clumsy and sexually illiterate child! On the other hand, while they said they did not need or

desire children for sex, they admitted that it was a wonderful sensual experience to be naked with a child and share body touch.

And I think this is an aspect that has never been really validated in the discussion of loving children. It could well be that a large amount of those accused of pedophilia *actually are searching for sensuality, not sexuality,* in their embracing a child, and that much here is actually a form of miscommunication and of emotional confusion. There is a certain probability that these men or women *have experienced sensuality in childhood only in an eroticized or even sexualized manner,* and within a codependent relationship with a parent, where typically emotions were experienced as entangled and confused.

What namely happens in codependent relationships where the parent considers the child as a partner replacement is that the borders between me and you are being blurred; the result is that the child is largely impeded from building a clear body image. And such *cofusion* counteracts to the child's natural striving for autonomy. The inevitable consequence of the confusion of body limits is that sensuality and sexuality are becoming confused and one is taken for

the other, or, more specifically, sexuality is sought after as a compensation for lacking sensuality. In other words, this means that natural and nonsexual touch that is nurturant and harmless is considered as 'sexual and harmful.'

Here, initial wrong conditioning can be changed using hypnotherapy or Gestalt therapy where the emphasis is put on relearning nonsexual body touch, emotional and physical closeness that is shared and sought after without a need for genital play and orgasm. But this reconditioning that a self-aware childlover could do as a *preventive measure* is almost rendered impossible in a society that does not value sensuality positively and that on its own metagroup level tends to confuse sensuality with sexuality.

For example, if a babysitter is jailed for having taken baths with the children or for having practiced childcare techniques known from aboriginal cultures, such as sleeping naked with the child, carrying the naked baby on the back, or given baby massage as it is known in India, then we face a meta-confusion, a confusion at the very root of our society.

This is, to repeat it, how this society, by its abhorrent lack of awareness and intelligent

permissiveness, breads violence and wrong behavior patterns by inducing in young people a lasting confusion between sensuality and sexuality.

Permissive education, if practiced consistently and as part of a new holistic governmental policy, could act counter to this widespread confusion and establish order in the community, and safety for children.

Chapter Two

Childlove and Normalcy

Some people forward the opinion that sexually all what is not adult-adult love is ultimately the result of some or the other form of inhibition or perversion, and that, thus, there was something like a concept of *normalcy* that says 'the best sex is the one between two adult and mature partners of different sexes.'

In personal correspondence, the person who wrote me this sentence came up with an extended and profit-based project for 'curing pedophiles' through exposing them to sexually highly experienced prostitutes in Thailand.

This guy, who is a fervent avatar of *logical reality*, intended to charge every prospect the sum of twenty thousand dollars for such a treatment.

I replied to him that I have formal objections against any such form of so-called therapy, and this

for well-founded ethical reasons. Let's not forget that such ideas abound in all fascist and totalitarian regimes and were an integral part of Hitler's euthanasia strategies.

This is what I have to object:

- Normalcy does not exist in nature;
- Normalcy is a left-brain concept, a pure intellectual construct;
- The formula *normalcy equals heterosexuality* follows the same bias;
- Heterosexuality is a cultural concept or idea, nothing real;
- Sexuality is not a fixated condition;
- Humans are not animals who follow instinctual conditioning;
- Human sexuality is not a self-executing drive;
- Human sexuality is not an automatism;
- Human sexuality is not distinct, not abstract from human emotions;

- Sex attraction follows emotional attraction, not *vice versa*;

- Sexual attraction cannot be split off from the individual person;

- Sexual attraction is part of the *soul continuum* of the person;

- Sexual attraction is invested with vital energy;

- Transforming a human being sexually is no solution;

- Transforming a human being sexually violates human dignity.

The argument that *ethical considerations are not relevant* when the person gives a valid consent is juridically not tenable as there are a matters so vital that they cannot be given to being consented to, as for example, *consenting to another killing oneself will not discharge the other from murder or manslaughter*, and here the same must apply as sexuality is an intrinsic part of a human life, whatever this sexuality is like.

Asking people to pay a huge sum of money for sexual transformation or changing on demand the

sexual conditioning is unethical in my view. In the case that full consent is present, it is still unethical when the money taken for such a treatment is exorbitant; besides there is little chance that the treatment will be effective.

While the sexual setup can well be changed in some cases so that a boylover may indeed be able to sleep with women, the more important *emotional attraction* that is at the basis of the sexual component will not be affected; thus the man will perhaps well sleep with girls but he will go out emotionally dissatisfied or even with a bad taste in the mouth because emotionally he still will feel attracted to boys; this is what feels *right* for him; thus the re-conditioning will rather have added to the discomfort of the person than to their comfort level.

This is so because emotional attraction that is, to repeat it, at the basis of sexual attraction, is not the result of conditioning; it has many origins, some being karmic, others being individual, and not all are involuntary; in fact some are the result of conscious choice. For example I can choose to care for children because I am against money and power, while I can see great good in taking care of children, especially in

a world that is so cruel to children in many societies. And I give a priority to my emotional attraction to children and say, for example, it counts more for me than social status and comfort or a high salary. I can then choose to become an educator for realizing my vision. At the basis of my decision is my emotional predilection for children. So this decision is based on an *emotional preference* and this in turn is based upon something we are hardly aware of, and that I call *soul values*. And then I go one step ahead and say that in certain cases and for reasons we do not yet really know, people develop a sexual attraction on top of their emotional preference, or as a result of it. Behold, not all people do, but certain well, and often without being conscious of it—until it's too late. The only solution here is not treatment, but *total acceptance* of our attractions, whatever they are; because this acceptance is the condition of a higher level of consciousness to develop.

When I replied with these arguments, the person wrote back:

> I believe the most fulfilling sexual experience any mature human is capable of even at an individual level (excluding certain genetic factors) is with a mature partner of the opposite sex.

And I replied further:

> As you stated at the very beginning, it's a belief. And I would even say nothing but a belief. In addition, no genetic factors conditioning human sexuality have ever been validly proven. They were all more or less part and parcel of terror regimes' doctoring people for social adjustment and thus, in terms of the Red Cross Conventions, exerting forms of torture. So-called scientific research based on such kind of soil cannot be trusted by any serious scientist. While one might argue that in view of body shape and size of genitals, two adult partners ideally fit in each other (while this is again an assumption because a petite girl being penetrated by a huge bulldog man may experience extreme pain) but not an adult and a child, the answer here is equally simple: not all in sexuality is teleological with the ultimate goal of (total) penetration; all is here subject to dialogue, to mutual bargain, to peaceful discussion, to trial-and-error over time, to play-like fun, and so on. And the ultimate satisfaction is not always and I would even say typically not the sexual satisfaction but the emotional satisfaction or the congruence between emotional and sexual fulfillment with one and the same partner.

This can well happen between an adult and a child, despite the obvious divergence in body size and genitals. I would even to as far as saying that the very fact of the existence of childlove shows that nature has not programmed us like machines that do sex as a robotic obsession so that, as it were, 'all fits in

each other.' We are not machines, we are human beings. We are more like cigars, hand-made and individually differently shaded, some coming with broken leaves, some having a different tint.

We are not cigarettes, machine-produced, every single piece like any other one, exactly the same. There is no straight line in nature, only in human intellectualism.

The compulsion to 'do sex' is a left-brain concept, a pure intellectual construct and it came up probably as an anti-reaction against patriarchal sex repression.

It also is part of the competition culture where sex is most of the time a *matter of performance* which makes that many men today are driven, time and again, into temporary, sporadic or even long-term impotence.

Chapter Three

When Law Punishes Life

Let us have a look what ages of consent are good for, or supposed to be good for! What is the idea behind segregating age groups and why is sexuality not allowed for all age groups? Why do laws almost everywhere rigidly fix certain ages for sex, and do not ask if sexual activity was constructive or damaging, peaceful or violent, coercive or consenting?

Law experts tend to argue that a precise age of consent assures legal clarity and certainty because in most cases it was not to make out if an individual child would experience sex positively or negatively.

Another argument brought forward by criminologists is that criminal law could not handle psychological questions and therefore needs to be clear-cut. I heard several of my lawyer colleagues advancing this argument that upon further inquiry

reveals to be barely correct. The true answer is that age of consent laws have *no rational basis at all*, and that their existence has merely historical reasons: they were the successors of *Canon Law*, that is Church law that preceded state law in all Western cultures.

Hence, the answer can only be found if we look at legal history, and inquire into how age-of-consent laws came about in the first place, what their original meaning was, and why they were at all introduced.

This inquiry is interesting because it will give the answer to the question why there was and will be no paradigm change in matters of sex legislation! This is so because the socioeconomic base layer for these laws is no more existing.

I have done this inquiry for the criminal law of the United States which is a common law jurisdiction; criminal laws vary from state to state and there is a large body of case law to help interpreting the statutes.

Sex laws are existing only since the beginning of patriarchy, and thus since around five thousand years. A marking event in history that usually is associated with the beginning of sex laws is the so-called *Code*

of Hammurabi, which probably for the first time in legal history contained a provision for the rape of a female child.

> —King Hammurabi (1792-1750 B.C.), sixth king of the Amorite Dynasty of Old Babylon, is considered as the avatar or even founder of patriarchy by most social historians. Hammurabi's Code of Laws is by far the earliest-known example of a ruler proclaiming publicly to his people an entire body of laws, arranged in orderly groups, so that all men might read and know what was required of them. This body of law was also the first in history that contained a compulsive rule on sexual behavior which was enforced by Draconian punishments, which regularly included violent beatings, torture, forced castration or even the death penalty.

Section 130 Code of Hammurabi

> If a man violate(s) the wife (betrothed or child-wife) of another man, who has never known a man, and still lives in her father's house, and sleep with her and be surprised, this man shall be put to death, but the wife is blameless.

From the wording, two interesting conclusions can be drawn. First, it was possible at this time that men married female children and consummated the marriage with them, second, the code did not want to protect the females but their male proprietor, an interpretation which is conclusive when looking at the origin of the word 'rape' in English, it namely comes

etymologically from Latin *rapus* and meant *theft*; the term originally had no connotation with sexuality. It was applied for the theft of human beings, as this was a common behavior in olden times for males to get a sex partner or even a spouse, just by 'stealing' a young boy or girl.

In most cases, those abductions however were of a temporary nature, as the child was taken back home after a fortnight. What is more, such cases did not end in a tragedy, as it is so common today when a child is abducted for sex.

In preceding cultures of which one was the matriarchal *Minoan Civilization* of Crete, the only sex taboo was incest in direct line, whereas otherwise there were no sexual restrictions. Notably, in this culture, the sexuality of children was completely free and looked at with a permissive attitude; this is still today the case with peaceful native cultures.

When we seriously wonder why we have sex laws and what they do in our society, or ought to do, we may realize how little our laws actually act against the madness-track that we are on as a society. What is the use of establishing laws based upon principles that, not only being irrational and largely out-of-date, were

put up against the laws of nature, and of love? At the end of the day we have endless prison miles filled with people who are in for their love or for having mishandled their vital energy. I am asking where the benefit of such lawmaking is for the betterment of society and the advancement of humanity and culture?

It is a fact that sex laws very clearly are preventing children from receiving various forms of body pleasure, despite the fact that, in the meantime, it is scientifically proven that *tactile and emotional deprivation creates havoc in children's psyche and immune system.*

My thirty years of research on sex laws involving children revealed that the rationale, or rather *irrationale*, behind these laws evidently is the alleged *sinful character of sex*, and not any possible destructive consequences of violence inflicted upon a child. This is not surprising since present sex laws are the remnants of a legal body created by the Christian Church, that was founded upon moralism rather than humanitarian, let alone bioenergetic principles.

At the time when the predecessors of our current age-of-consent laws were drafted, the child as a

person had no legal status; children's legal status was derived from the legal status of their father. It is very important to keep this in mind when reviewing present age-of-consent laws for they were drafted originally from this perspective, and not from our perspective as 21st century citizens with our focus on the child's ultimate welfare.

This is particularly important when we deal with terms such as 'sexual purity,' 'innocence,' 'decency,' 'modesty,' 'moral conduct' or 'moral integrity' for these terms actually let us see that the object of protection is not the child or the child's physical integrity, but a societal, cultural, ideal or religious value such as *morality*—whatever this is.

And whatever it is, it shouldn't be of relevance for a modern lawmaker in a democracy that wants to mark a difference to fundamentalist horror regimes.

While the sexual purity or innocence of a child is historically *a relatively recent idea*, and while this idea may have some importance within the Christian value system, *the mass media today seem to suggest that we deal in so far with a biological or psychological truth.*

—See Unlawful Sex (1985), 4.3, p. 20.

And this despite the fact that progressive child psychologists such as Alayne Yates clearly state that a child's sexual purity is a pure myth. Despite that, our outdated sexual laws take it for granted that a child has to be protected from experiencing the most pleasurable side of life.

—See Alayne Yates, Sex Without Shame (1978).

Many a brutal attack against a child is performed by parents or educators exactly because children act against the innocence terror imposed upon them by an anti-life culture, and actively pursue to have sex with peers or adults they love. And how ferocious punishments tend to be for this truly innocent reason, and how disproportionate they regularly are, is a matter of common knowledge. Alexander S. Neill, founder of *Summerhill School* in England reports in his book such an incident following sex play he had as a boy with his sister.

—See in A.S. Neill's autobiography Neill! Neill! Orange-Peel! (1972). The traumatic effects of such early punishment for sex play and its lasting influence on the personality of the later adult have since long been discovered by psychoanalysis.

LOVE OR LAWS?

Sex laws are among the most hilarious perversities in our whole legal body. When girls were only sexually mature at around 14 in the Middle Ages, they could consent to sex from age 10.

Later, when puberty occurred at about 12 years of age, the consent of girls under 16 was considered legally invalid. Today, in the Western world, *puberty happens between ten and twelve years of age* because of highly potent and hormone-rich nutrition, but a fifteen-year old girl cannot make love with her older boyfriend without the boy risking to be charged with statutory rape.

What is the point of such legal nonsense?

The fact is that there is no logic in sex laws because *they are not made on the basis of rational reasoning* but reflect irrational moralistic ideas that originate from non-legal sources: church law, folk wisdom, superstition and a more or less total ignorance about physical love as it is so typical for Western culture as a whole.

What these laws do is to kill life and pervert man into a beast that has spoiled its natural and innocent sexuality, replacing it by a mix of sex-plus-violence

that makes him a highly dangerous creature. The proscription of love, as we defined it as being mutually consenting sexual activity between humans regardless of age, is likely to cause psychosomatic disease, and generally turns man into an aggressive individual.

So, for everybody who has some common sense left, it should become clear that those laws have to be revised or, best, abandoned if humanity is to survive into a less violent and peaceful era.

Statutory Rape

Three precedents by the *Supreme Court of Arkansas* in 1891, 1897 and 1904 show evicently how *statutory rape* came to be recognized as a legal term.

While, according to an early English statute, the original rule incorporated in American common law was 'if any person shall unlawfully and carnally know and abuse any woman-child under the age of ten years, it shall be a felony without clergy,' the courts have extended more and more the term abuse of a woman-child.

—Wharton's Criminal Law (1979), § 291, p. 43.

In a 1891 case, *Warner v. State*, the *Supreme Court of Arkansas* still distinguished between rape as non-consenting intercourse which was punishable with death, and the carnal and unlawful knowledge of a female child under the age of puberty which was punishable between 5 and 21 years in the penitentiary. (54 Ark 660, 17 SW 6)

The court stated that '[t]he crime of carnally knowing a female child under the age of puberty can be committed only when the victim is under 12 years old, and has sufficient intelligence to know the nature of the act, and to consent, and does consent thereto.'

According to an earlier decision of the same court (Coates v. State (1888), 7 SW 304), puberty was deemed to begin with 12 years of age. In the case, the girl had been 11-years old and the accused had offered proof as to her consenting to intercourse.

In the 1897 case, *Bond v. State*, a new statute was considered which made punishable carnal knowledge of a girl under 16 years of age with or without her consent. (63 Ark 504, 39 SW 554) Thus, the distinction between *forcible rape* (intercourse without consent)

and *consenting intercourse*, which was still a basis of the 1891 precedent, was abandoned by the new statute.

The result was that forcible rape, which means sexual violence, became assimilated with consenting intercourse! Even without looking at consequences of such an abstruse legal situation, from a legal policy point of view, it's not only nonsense, but forbidden to do that as a legislator. It's against all and every rule of sound legal policy!

It had two consequences. Firstly, the former ultimate punishment in form of the death penalty for forcible rape was lowered to the punishment of statutory rape (5 to 21 years penitentiary). Thus, the rapist of an adult woman was punished much harder than the rapist of a girl under sixteen!

Secondly, consenting intercourse with girls between ages 12 and 16 became, for the first time in history, a crime! This is strange because the courts affirmed that puberty was happening at age twelve whereas under the former liberal common law maturity happened much later. Thus the question remains open what in fact the new statute was to protect if not a pure morality principle?!

In the 1904 case, *Plunkett v. State*, the *Supreme Court of Arkansas* used for the first time the new legal term *statutory rape* which is per definition no rape, but a consenting sexual activity, legally deemed as being a rape-like offense. (72 Ark 409, 82 SW 845)

In the case the girl had been fifteen, had consented to intercourse and had born a baby. It was not certain that the accused was the father of the baby. But on a charge for statutory rape evidence that the girl had had sexual intercourse also with other men was *not admissible!*

Thus, even if the girl had had regular sexual intercourse with other men and the baby had been from another man, the accused would not have been able to construe a defense from this fact.

This again shows that what the new law of statutory rape actually protected was some dubious notion of 'public morals,' but not the corporal integrity of a child.

This is furthermore corroborated by the fact that the statute only punished unlawful sexual intercourse, that is intercourse outside a valid marriage. At the time, girls could notably marry at age fourteen. Thus,

had the accused married the girl before the intercourse happened, sex would have been lawful under the statute and no punishment had resulted from the intercourse. So what, in fact, has all this to do with rape and sexual violence?

In addition, laws in this area are of a vagueness that must be a thorn in the eye of any sincere legal expert.

We have seen that rape and statutory rape are two distinct offenses and that statutory rape has nothing to do with the forcible penetration of the female sexual organ against her will, but that it typically is a *consenting sexual activity* between two persons of different age. It is therefore pure sophism and against the constitutional principle of *due process* to classify it as a rape-like act. The annotated and revised Arizona Statutes collection notes:

Ariz Rev Stats Ann, § 13-1401(3)

> Viewed conceptually, a female under a specified age is also deemed incapable of consenting and hence her apparent consent is treated as immaterial.

Not enough with this legal mess, certain states also extended the term 'sexual intercourse' to

encompass 'any manual masturbatory contact with the penis or vulva' (Arizona).

> —Wharton's Criminal Law (1979), § 293, p. 65 citing Code Ga Ann, § 26-2019 and § 298, pp. 105 ff.

In good English, not only when the older boyfriend sleeps with our 15-year old, but already when he caresses manually her vaginal lips, and when they do this in Arizona, he has raped her in Arizona—statutorily, but nonetheless. *Viewed conceptually!*

CHILD MOLESTATION AND ABUSE

In Georgia, another rape like offense is called *child molestation:*

> A person commits child molestation, with imprisonment from one to twenty years, when 'he does any immoral or indecent act to or in the presence of or with any child under the age of fourteen years with the intent to arouse or satisfy the sexual desires of either the child or the person.
>
> —It is equally sufficient that the child touches the clothing covering the immediate area of the adult's intimate parts, see Wharton's Criminal Law (1979), § 298, p. 106.

In good English, someone who touches a child's genitals, or let his genitals touch by a child, or shows the child how to masturbate, even if this person is the child's parent, in Georgia goes to prison for twenty years at maximum. For, *viewed conceptually*, the child has been 'raped' *by the sex knowledge* received through such teaching.

This is only one of many examples that demonstrate that it is not the child that is protected by such laws, but the perpetuation of adult sexual inhibitions and a *totally corrupt and perverted morality!* It is a crime worth twenty years of prison to show a child having sexual pleasure.

In addition, it is a crime to *masturbate for hire*, which means to stimulate the sexual organs of a client by a masseur or masseuse.

—Wharton's Criminal Law (1979), § 300, p. 112.

In Iowa, the sexual contact with a child is a 'lascivious act with a child,' in Illinois it is 'indecent liberties with a child' or 'contributing to the sexual delinquency of a child.'

—Id., § 297, p. 92 and § 300, p. 113.

This latter formulation is particularly significant. Not only that human sexuality destroys children and animals, it also renders children 'delinquent.'

The very contrary is true, as was shown by Alexander S. Neill in *Summerhill* and other free schools and by Paul Goodman in their work with delinquent adolescents: it is exactly the *denial*, imposed by an emotionally and sexually frigid society, to love, to live their budding sexuality in a healthy way which contributes essentially to their getting on a wrong path.

Our sex laws, our sex trials and our correction system are a modern copy of the Church's Inquisition and have very little to do with a modern penal law system.

They are an what I call *legislative perversion*.

And the question is if a society with such an aggression level has a mandate at all for protecting children against physical or sexual violence, for *it is itself based upon nothing but violence!*

The perversity of these laws becomes particularly evident when one compares them with the jurisprudence on corporal punishment that reveals

how little this same society cares about the pain and the suffering inflicted upon a child 'in the name of its own good.' To tear up the skin of a small child with a whip, to blow the naked bottom of a child with a stick is lawful; to lick it tenderly is qualified as 'anilingus' and is a criminal offense equated with sexual penetration, deviate intercourse or sodomy, and worth twenty years of jail.

—Wharton's Criminal Law (1979), § 297.

Wait a moment, what appears truly *deviate* here is the value system of a society that punishes innocent natural pleasure and worships violence, perversion and brutality!

In addition, let me mention the fact that violence against the child is endorsed by social custom that lets children fight in martial arts competitions, for which parents and educators actively encourage children. These competitions are *violent*, they are not just *playful* or *entertaining*.

Children are fought into submission. The fact that it is in a controlled environment with rules makes no difference. What is more dangerous for children, receiving sexual instruction from an adult that will

benefit their erotic intelligence and wellbeing, or being face to face with another child in an *organized fight competition* where the child risks *minor, moderate or serious injuries* including broken bones, blood shed, emotional and physiological trauma?

LAW REFORM

The history of sexual laws involving children can clearly be retraced in the Netherlands. It was briefly outlined by Dr. Edward Brongersma, Dutch lawyer and Senator, in his Berlin University course, in 1981.

> —This and the following information about the Dutch sexual law reforms have kindly been provided by Dr. Edward Brongersma, at the time Senator of the Dutch House of Lords, and himself involved in the reforms as a parliamentary member. The information was given to me as a script entitled Der Speijer-Report, 1981 (in German language) that Dr. Brongersma had originally drafted for a lecture at Berlin University, Germany.

Until 1886 sex with children of both sexes was not punishable in the Netherlands, in France until 1832. Homosexuality was punishable with the death penalty, but only in the *ecclesiastical courts*, which is the courts that applied *Canon Law*, the body of law established by the Christian Church.

The same is true for the common law, with regard to sodomy.

> —See Wharton's Criminal Law (1979), §§ 294 ff. It is typical for the Christian Church's act-centered mechanistic view of sexuality that sexual behavior was judged and classified by the 'acts' performed, and not as a physical form of human love. As a result, in common law, sodomy was defined in accordance to the former ecclesiastical laws (canon law) from which it had been adopted as the 'carnal copulation of persons in other than the natural manner,' i.e. in a way which was against nature (see Wharton's Criminal Law, § 295, p. 77). Needless to mention that it was the Church who defined what was 'nature' and what was not.

Contrary to the Church's Inquisition laws, Montesquieu wrote in *L'Esprit des Lois* that society should only punish behavior that was damaging to its members, and not what was only against certain moral rules.

From 1810 to 1886 the Netherlands' civil law statute was a translation of the French *Code Napoléon* under which nonviolent intercourse was not punishable regardless of the sex and age of the partners! Only after 1886, in the Netherlands' first own penal code, *Het Wetboek van Strafrecht*, an age of consent of 14 years was introduced. The proposed 14 years as the age of consent became 16 years in the

parliamentary discussions. A minority in the *House of Commons* used the opportunity to propose punishment for homosexuality. But the majority refused: no moralizing in the penal code. But this was only until 1911.

A catholic minister of justice finally was powerful enough to change the situation and penalize homosexuality. This is the way laws are made.

It is interesting that a socialist M.P. remarked at that time: 'One day we'll have to regret this, for homosexuality is not damaging.' But this law was only for homosexual acts with persons under twenty-one years. It was the Nazis who, during their occupancy in the Netherlands made punishable homosexuality among adults. The Dutch parliament, according to Brongersma, did never accept this and declared later to deem this law as being non-existent.

This went on until 1968 when the *Speijer-Report* was drafted in which all myths about homosexuality were disproved with profound scientific references. *Inter alia*, it was stated that since it was eventually accepted knowledge that children are sexual, the opinion grew that the dangers from sexual encounters for children and adolescents have been

overestimated. In its conclusion, the expert commission stated that 'seduction' did not play the role that most people attributed to it; they said that even in cases where the adult initiated the child in the sexual activity, the child in many cases awaited from the adult to be initiated.

This was found to be true for both homosexual and heterosexual encounters between children and adults. Finally it was stated that initiation, in what sexual direction whatever it led, could in many cases contribute to a more mental and physical sanity, and no to depravement.

Behold, all this is stated in an official document of the Dutch government. The Minister of Justice at this time, Polak, supported the report and made it a basis for a legal reform draft. The draft was so convincing that in the 2nd Chamber of the Dutch House of Commons only 5 members out of 150 had voted against it—these were from the ultra right-wing part of the political spectrum. The Dutch House of Lords adopted the draft bill unanimously.

In October 1969, the Dutch parliament, according to the Speijer-Report, abolished the law which discriminated homosexual pedophilia thus fixing 16

years as the appropriate age of consent for man-boy sexual relations, which was formerly 21 years. In most countries, the discrimination of homosexual pedophilia is still existing, yet the ages of consent differ.

In England, the *Indecency with Children Act 1960* makes punishable any act of indecency, or incitement to indecency, with or towards a child under 14, regardless of the sex of either the child or the offender. In addition, and to repeat it, homosexual relationships were prohibited with persons under 21 years of age. *The Policy Advisory Committee on Sexual Offenses (1981)* has recommended that this age should be reduced to 18.

—See Unlawful Sex (1985), 8.26 and 8.29.

It is similar in Germany where the general age of consent is equated with the legal definition of 'child' (person under 14 years of age), while there is a discrimination according to the nature of the relationship: 14 years (§ 176 StGB), 16 in ascendancy relations, 18 in dependency relations (§ 174 StGB) and 18 for homosexual acts (§ 175 StGB).

—Dreher/Tröndle, Strafgesetzbuch und Nebengesetze (1985), §§ 174 ff.

In France, nonviolent indecent attacks (attentat à la pudeur sans violence) on a child under 15 years is punishable according to art. 331, al. 1er and 3 Code Pénal, but also nonviolent indecent acts on minors between 15 and 18 years if ascendancy relations are in question (Art. 331–1). Equally homosexual acts with a minor between 15 and 18 years of age are punishable (Art. 331– 2).

> —See, for example, Roger Merle, André Vitu, Traité de Droit Criminel (1982), pp. 1510 ff.

In Denmark, the age of consent is 15 for both sexes, without any further discrimination of homosexual acts.

In Switzerland, the age of consent is 16, but there is much criticism in the literature on this age of consent and proposals are made to fix 14 years as a more appropriate age limit. Besides that, however, so-called homosexual seduction is even punishable with persons above 16 years of age.

> —See Günter Stratenwerth, Schweizerisches Strafrecht (1984), pp. 28, 29. The same article (§ 191) cf the Swiss Penal Code encompasses both dependency and ascendancy relations as qualifications in punishment.

The Dutch legislation, too, foresees a protection clause for homosexual relationships with minors over 16 years of age. Such relations are still punishable when the prosecution can prove 'relevant danger to the child' that was a consequence of the homosexual act and that would not have occurred in a heterosexual encounter.

However, such cases will be extremely rare. The scientific research upon which the Speijer-Report was based revealed that by the 16th year of life, the sexual propensity is developed to such an extent that a youngster who is heterosexual cannot be diverted by seduction into permanent homosexuality.

—Unlawful Sex (1985), 4.17.

In practice, the prosecution and police forces from that time until the 1990s refused in about 66% of all cases to file a criminal action for adults involved in an erotic relation with children beyond the age of 12.

After the fundamentalist fascist drift in the Netherlands in 1996, as a consequence of American pressure and the worldwide public child abuse hysteria, however, the situation has changed very much for the worse.

Still in 1981, a petition of the association of the work group for pedophilia and of the greatest Dutch association of primary school teachers was presented to the Dutch government aiming at the total abandonment of all age of consent in sex laws.

Another petition was presented in 1987 to the Dutch Minister of Justice proposing to specify conditions under which the prohibition did not apply, *notably in those cases in which the child initiates or actively engages in the sexual activity*. The petition was signed by a considerable number of persons including law professors, lawyers, prosecution attorneys, physicians, psychologists, psychiatrists, psychotherapists, sociologists, youth workers, priests or authors, and was a representative sample of the Dutch society.

Moreover, the recommendations of the *Advisory Committee on Moral Legislation (Melai Committee)*, which were published in 1980, and the draft of a bill, presented to the Dutch cabinet in 1985 are worth to be mentioned. The Melai-Report proposed that the prohibition of sex with persons under 16 years of age, that however excluded dependency relations, should be changed into a prohibition of *sexual*

rapprochement of such persons, which means that the report only wanted to punish pimps or brothels, or people who engage in a sex business involving children.

The draft bill of 1985 contained a prohibition of sexual contacts with below 16-year olds that have been prepared or promoted by presenting or promising gifts, abuse of ascendancy or by deception.

This decriminalization would only apply in non-dependency relations. Thus, incest with children under 16 would remain entirely forbidden. At present the age limit for incest is twenty-one.

> —Dr. Jan Schujer, Ministry of Interior, The Hague, Netherlands, kindly provided this information regarding the content of those petitions and the legal draft projects.

As in the Netherlands, the debate in France, Denmark, Germany and Switzerland and other countries went on over years as to lowering the age of consent from sixteen to fourteen years of age. Compared with the previous state of the laws however, that is, before the 19th century, a single lowering of the age of consent seems to be dysfunctional in that it looks like 'propaganda for

progressiveness' rather than a real effort for drafting more rational criminal laws. After all, we have to ask where is the justification for age fourteen? Why not thirteen, twelve or eleven?

The question is if an age of consent has any rationale at all? At least, when fixing the age at the age of puberty, one could argue that puberty or sexual maturity is a biological event that can be considered a justifiable landmark for reform drafts concerning the age of consent.

Love Reform

After these rather tedious details, I would like to focus on our initial question *Love or Laws?* and ask if we were not completely mistaken to engage in law reform rather than thinking about reforming our relationship with love?

This sounds perhaps frivolous but is not meant to be; my perspective and effort for a new solution is serious and not just a leisure occupation. I have now researched on these topics for exactly twenty-four years, as I did my first basic research in Spring 1985, and have invested considerable time, energy and

resources to get a rather precise idea of how this paradigm change in matters of human sexuality is to come about.

For most feminist authors, the idea of a basically new societal attitude regarding love and sexuality is surely a point on their agenda. Nobody doubts this. And yet, when we rest with ideological positions, a larger perspective of truth seems to precluded, as we will stay with our particular bias, as feminists, as homosexuals, as pedophiles or as sensation-hungry journalists.

I think it is significant that my first research study was rejected by *Global Academic Publishers*, a boylove editor in the United States and Netherlands who namely published Dr. Brongersma's books. They thought my views were not radical enough and too much on the line of feminist ideas. Myself not being addicted to feminism, the reply of the editor surprised me, but it showed me to what extent most people think in established categories, unable to view life, and problems, from different angles. Truly, I do not need to be a feminist to correctly report what feminist authors think and write on a certain topic. And when I just leave it out from my study because I don't like

feminism, I am not a scientific author, but a pamphlet smearer or boulevard press reporter.

And in fact, I think we are clearly in an impasse once we begin to reform impossible laws, laws that were basically made during times of extreme irrationality and by highly violent secular or religiously fundamentalist governments of the past, and that in many respects violate our most cherished constitutional guarantees!

When we see that, we are perhaps able to do that paradigm change right now, in our own consciousness, by looking differently at the problem or our basic question. What do we want? Love? Or Laws?

What do we need in a future society that will be based on rational and freedom-loving principles and that respects the individual and trusts the citizen? Is it more and more laws?

Behold, I am not preaching a gospel here and I do not talk about an idealist principle. I am in fact against idealism and ideals because they are truly destructive, as Krishnamurti has shown, and because they have contributed a great deal to the present chaos of

violence, superficial and blindfolding entertainment, environmental pollution and the ruthless massacre of many of our most precious native cultures.

When we talk about love, we do not talk about an ideal. Love is an energy that is all-present in the cosmos; love in all its forms, also as physical love, is part of life, of energy, and not a mental concept. And as such, it is *reality*, do what you will! Thus, when I talk about love, I talk about reality, the reality of nature, or of the universe. And this has been proven, in the meantime, by quantum physics, and that is by itself a major scientific paradigm shift that throws us, if we want it or not, into the holistic science paradigm of the 21st century.

When we are at all serious as scientists, or as childcare professionals or child psychologists, lawyers or judges we cannot continue to close our eyes in front of children's *emotional, tactile and sexual needs*, and we cannot continue absolving society for mutilating the child's emotional and sexual wholeness and transforming children into schizoid personalities through the collective denial of their most basic and important emotions. And we cannot continue to justify *abhorrently unjust, irrational and perverse laws*

with the smeary and non-verifiable argument they 'protected' our children. While we know for sure that the best protection is freedom, and love!

BIBLIOGRAPHY

Contextual Bibliography

Abrams, Jeremiah (Ed.)

Reclaiming the Inner Child
New York: Tarcher/Putnam, 1990

Alston, John P. / Tucker, Francis

The Myth of Sexual Permissiveness
The Journal of Sex Research, 9/1 (1973)

Appleton, Matthew

A Free Range Childhood
Self-Regulation at Summerhill School
Foundation for Educational Renewal, 2000

Ariès, Philippe

L'Enfant et la Famille sous l'Ancien Régime
Paris, Seuil, 1975

Centuries of Childhood
New York: Vintage Books, 1962

BACHOFEN, JOHANN JAKOB

GESAMMELTE WERKE, BAND 2
Das Mutterrecht
Basel: Benno Schwabe & Co, 1948
First published in 1861

BAGLEY, CHRISTOPHER

CHILD ABUSERS
Research and Treatment
New York: Universal Publishers, 2003

BARBAREE, HOWARD E. & MARSHALL, WILLIAM L. (EDS.)

THE JUVENILE SEX OFFENDER
Second Edition
New York: Guilford Press, 2008

BENDER LAURETTA & BLAU, ABRAM

THE REACTION OF CHILDREN TO SEXUAL RELATIONS WITH ADULTS
American J. Orthopsychiatry 7 (1937), 500-518

BERNARD, FRITS

PAEDOPHILIA
A Factual Report
Amsterdam: Enclave, 1985

BRANT & TISZA

THE SEXUALLY MISUSED CHILD
American J. Orthopsychiatry, 47(1)(1977)

BRONGERSMA, EDWARD

AGGRESSION AGAINST PEDOPHILES
7 International Journal of Law & Psychiatry 82 (1984)

LOVING BOYS (VOL.1 & VOL. 2)
Amsterdam, New York: Global Academic Publishers, 1987

BULLOUGH & BULLOUGH (EDS.)

HUMAN SEXUALITY
An Encyclopedia
New York: Garland Publishing, 1994

SIN, SICKNESS AND SANITY
A History of Sexual Attitudes
New York: New American Library, 1977

BURGESS, ANN WOLBERT

CHILD PORNOGRAPHY AND SEX RINGS
New York: Lexington Books, 1984

BUXTON, RICHARD

THE COMPLETE WORLD OF GREEK MYTHOLOGY
London: Thames & Hudson, 2007

CAIN, CHELSEA & MOON UNIT ZAPPA

WILD CHILD
New York: Seal Press (Feminist Publishing), 1999

Calderone & Ramey

Talking With Your Child About Sex
New York: Random House, 1982

Campbell, Herbert James

The Pleasure Areas
London: Eyre Methuen Ltd., 1973

Campbell, Jacqueline C.

Assessing Dangerousness
Violence by Sexual Offenders, Batterers and Child Abusers
New York: Sage Publications, 2004

Chaplin, Charles

My Autobiography
New York: Plume, 1992
Originally published in 1964

Clarke-Steward, S., Friedman, S. & Koch, J.

Child Development, A Topical Approach
London: John Wiley, 1986

Constantine, Larry L.

Children & Sex
New Findings, New Perspectives
Larry L. Constantine & Floyd M. Martinson (Eds.)
Boston: Little, Brown & Company, 1981

BIBLIOGRAPHY

Treasures of the Island
Children in Alternative Lifestyles
Beverly Hills: Sage Publications, 1976

Where are the Kids?
in: Libby & Whitehurst (ed.)
Marriage and Alternatives
Glenview: Scott Foresman, 1977

Open Family
A Lifestyle for Kids and other People
26 FAMILY COORDINATOR 113-130 (1977)

Cook, M. & Howells, K. (Eds.)

Adult Sexual Interest in Children
Academic Press, London, 1980

Covitz, Joel

Emotional Child Abuse
The Family Curse
Boston: Sigo Press, 1986

Currier, Richard L.

Juvenile Sexuality in Global Perspective
in : Children & Sex, New Findings, New Perspectives
Larry L. Constantine & Floyd M. Martinson (Eds.)
Boston: Little, Brown & Company, 1981

DeMause, Lloyd

The History of Childhood
New York, 1974

FOUNDATIONS OF PSYCHOHISTORY
New York: Creative Roots, 1982

EDWARDES, A.

THE JEWEL OF THE LOTUS
New York, 1959

EISLER, RIANE

THE CHALICE AND THE BLADE
Our history, Our future
San Francisco: Harper & Row, 1995

SACRED PLEASURE: SEX, MYTH AND THE POLITICS OF THE BODY
New Paths to Power and Love
San Francisco: Harper & Row, 1996

ELLIS, HAVELOCK

SEXUAL INVERSION
New York: University Press of the Pacific, 2001
Originally published in 1897.

ELWIN, V.

THE MURIA AND THEIR GHOTUL
Bombay: Oxford University Press, 1947

ERIKSON, ERIK H.

CHILDHOOD AND SOCIETY
New York: Norton, 1993
First published in 1950

BIBLIOGRAPHY

Farson, Richard

Birthrights
A Bill of Rights for Children
Macmillan, New York, 1974

Finkelhor, David

Sexually Victimized Children
New York: Free Press, 1981

Fortune, Mary M.

Sexual Violence
New York: Pilgrim Press, 1994

Foster/Freed

A Bill of Rights for Children
6 FAMILY LAW QUARTERLY 343 (1972)

Foucault, Michel

The History of Sexuality, Vol. I : The Will to Knowledge
London: Penguin, 1998
First published in 1976

The History of Sexuality, Vol. II : The Use of Pleasure
London: Penguin, 1998
First published in 1984

The History of Sexuality, Vol. III : The Care of Self
London: Penguin, 1998
First published in 1984

Freud, Anne

War and Children
London, 1943.

Freund, Kurt

Assessment of Pedophilia
in: Cook, M. and Howells, K. (eds.)
Adult Sexual Interest in Children
Academic Press, London, 1980

Fromm, Erich

The Anatomy of Human Destructiveness
New York: Owl Book, 1992
Originally published in 1973

Escape from Freedom
New York: Owl Books, 1994
Originally published in 1941

To Have or To Be
New York: Continuum International Publishing, 1996
Originally published in 1976

The Art of Loving
New York: HarperPerennial, 2000
Originally published in 1956

Geldard, Richard

Remembering Heraclitus
New York: Lindisfarne Books, 2000

GIL, DAVID G.

SOCIETAL VIOLENCE AND VIOLENCE IN FAMILIES
in: David G. Gil, Child Abuse and Violence
New York: Ams Press, 1928

GOLDSTEIN, JEFFREY H.

AGGRESSION AND CRIMES OF VIOLENCE
New York, 1975

GORDON, ROSEMARY

PEDOPHILIA: NORMAL AND ABNORMAL
in: Kraemer, The Forbidden Love
London, 1976

GROTH, A. NICHOLAS

MEN WHO RAPE
The Psychology of the Offender
New York: Perseus Publishing, 1980

GUNN, JOHN

VIOLENCE
New York/Washington, 1973

HÉROARD, JEAN

JOURNAL DE JEAN HÉROARD SUR L'ENFANCE ET LA JEUNESSE DE LOUIS XIII
Paris: Soul/Barthélemy, 1868

HOWELLS, KEVIN

ADULT SEXUAL INTEREST IN CHILDREN
Considerations Relevant to Theories of Aetiology in:
Cook, M. and Howells, K. (eds.): Adult Sexual Interest in Children
Academic Press, London, 1980

HOOD, J.X.

SEXUAL CURIOSITIES OF LOVE, SEX AND MARRIAGE
A Survey of Sex Relations, Beliefs and Customs of Mankind in Different Countries and Ages
New York, 1951

JACKSON, STEVI

CHILDHOOD AND SEXUALITY
New York: Blackwell, 1982

JOHNSTON & DEISHER

CONTEMPORARY COMMUNAL CHILD REARING: A FIRST ANALYSIS
52 PEDIATRICS 319 (1973)

JONES, W.H.S., LITT, D.

PLINY NATURAL HISTORY
Cambridge, Mass.: Harvard University Press, 1980

KRAEMER

THE FORBIDDEN LOVE
London, 1976

BIBLIOGRAPHY

Krafft-Ebing, Richard von

Psychopathia Sexualis
New York: Bell Publishing, 1965
Originally published in 1886

Laud, Anne & Gilstrop, May

Violence in the Family
A Selected Bibliography on Child Abuse, Sexual Abuse of Children & Domestic Violence, June 1985, University of Georgia Libraries, Bibliographical Series, No. 32

Licht, Hans

Sexual Life in Ancient Greece
New York: AMS Press, 1995

Liedloff, Jean

Continuum Concept
In Search of Happiness Lost
New York: Perseus Books, 1986
First published in 1977

Locke, John

Some Thoughts Concerning Education
London, 1690
Reprinted in: The Works of John Locke, 1823
Vol. IX., pp. 6-205

LOWEN, ALEXANDER

DEPRESSION AND THE BODY
The Biological Basis of Faith and Reality
New York: Penguin, 1992

FEAR OF LIFE
New York: Bioenergetic Press, 2003

HONORING THE BODY
The Autobiography of Alexander Lowen
New York: Bioenergetic Press, 2004

JOY
The Surrender to the Body and to Life
New York: Penguin, 1995

LOVE AND ORGASM
New York: Macmillan, 1965

LOVE, SEX AND YOUR HEART
New York: Bioenergetics Press, 2004

NARCISSISM: DENIAL OF THE TRUE SELF
New York: Macmillan, Collier Books, 1983

PLEASURE: A CREATIVE APPROACH TO LIFE
New York: Bioenergetics Press, 2004
First published in 1970

THE LANGUAGE OF THE BODY
Physical Dynamics of Character Structure
New York: Bioenergetics Press, 2006

MALINOWSKI, BRONISLAW

CRIME UND CUSTOM IN SAVAGE SOCIETY
London: Kegan, 1926

BIBLIOGRAPHY

SEX AND REPRESSION IN SAVAGE SOCIETY
London: Kegan, 1927

THE SEXUAL LIFE OF SAVAGES IN NORTH WEST MELANESIA
New York: Halycon House, 1929

MANN, EDWARD W.

ORGONE, REICH & EROS
Wilhelm Reich's Theory of Life Energy
New York: Simon & Schuster (Touchstone), 1973

MARTINSON, FLOYD M.

SEXUAL KNOWLEDGE
Values and Behavior Patterns
St. Peter: Minn.: Gustavus Adolphus College, 1966

INFANT AND CHILD SEXUALITY
St. Peter: Minn.: Gustavus Adolphus College, 1973

THE QUALITY OF ADOLESCENT EXPERIENCES
St. Peter: Minn.: Gustavus Adolphus College, 1974

THE CHILD AND THE FAMILY
Calgary, Alberta: The University of Calgary, 1980

THE SEX EDUCATION OF YOUNG CHILDREN
in: Lorna Brown (Ed.), Sex Education in the Eighties
New York, London: Plenum Press, 1981, pp. 51 ff.

THE SEXUAL LIFE OF CHILDREN
New York: Bergin & Garvey, 1994

CHILDREN AND SEX, PART II: CHILDHOOD SEXUALITY
in: Bullough & Bullough, Human Sexuality (1994)
Pp. 111-116

Masters, R.E.L.

Forbidden Sexual Behavior and Morality
New York, 1962

Mead, Margaret

Sex and Temperament in Three Primitive Societies
New York, 1935

Miller, Alice

Four Your Own Good
Hidden Cruelty in Child-Rearing and the Roots of Violence
New York: Farrar, Straus & Giroux, 1983

Pictures of a Childhood
New York: Farrar, Straus & Giroux, 1986

The Drama of the Gifted Child
In Search for the True Self
translated by Ruth Ward
New York: Basic Books, 1996

Thou Shalt Not Be Aware
Society's Betrayal of the Child
New York: Noonday, 1998

The Political Consequences of Child Abuse
in: The Journal of Psychohistory 26, 2 (Fall 1998)

Moll, Albert

The Sexual Life of the Child
New York: Macmillan, 1912
First published in German as
Das Sexualleben des Kindes, 1909

MONTER, W. WILLIAM

WITCHCRAFT IN FRANCE AND SWITZERLAND
Ithaca & London: Cornell University Press, 1976

MONTAGU, ASHLEY

TOUCHING
The Human Significance of the Skin
New York: Harper & Row, 1978

MONTESSORI, MARIA

THE ABSORBENT MIND
Reprint Edition
New York: Buccaneer Books, 1995
First published in 1973

MOORE, THOMAS

CARE OF THE SOUL
A Guide for Cultivating Depth and Sacredness in Everyday Life
New York: Harper & Collins, 1994

MOSER, CHARLES ALLEN

DSM-IV-TR AND THE PARAPHILIAS: AN ARGUMENT FOR REMOVAL
With Peggy J. Kleinplatz
Journal of Psychology and Human Sexuality 17 (3/4), 91-109 (2005)

MURDOCK, G.

SOCIAL STRUCTURE
New York: Macmillan, 1960

Neill, Alexander Sutherland

Neill! Neill! Orange-Peel!
New York: Hart Publishing Co., 1972

Summerhill
A Radical Approach to Child Rearing
New York: Hart Publishing, Reprint 1984
Originally published 1960

Summerhill School
A New View of Childhood
New York: St. Martin's Press
Reprint 1995

O'Brian, Shirley

Child Pornography
2nd Edition
New York: Kendall/Hunt, 1992

Patridge, Burgo

History of Orgies
New York, 1960.

Plummer, Kenneth

Pedophilia
Constructing a Sociological Baseline
in: in: Cook, M. and Howells, K. (Eds.):
Adult Sexual Interest in Children
Academic Press, London, 1980, pp. 220 ff.

BIBLIOGRAPHY

Porteous, Hedy S.

Sex and Identity
Your Child's Sexuality
Indianapolis: Bobbs-Merrill, 1972

Prescott, James W.

Body Pleasure and the Origins of Violence
Bulletin of the Atomic Scientists, 10-20 (1975)

Deprivation of Physical Affection as a Primary Process in the Development of Physical Violence A Comparative and Cross-Cultural Perspective, in: David G. Gil, ed., Child Abuse and Violence
New York: Ams Press, 1979

Pritchard, Colin

The Child Abusers
New York: Open University Press, 2004

Reich, Wilhelm

Children of the Future
On the Prevention of Sexual Pathology
New York: Farrar, Straus & Giroux, 1983
First published in 1950

The Function of the Orgasm (The Orgone, Vol. 1)
Orgone Institute Press, New York, 1942

The Invasion of Compulsory Sex Morality
New York: Farrar, Straus & Giroux, 1971
Originally published in 1932

The Sexual Revolution
©1945, 1962 by Mary Boyd Higgins as Director of the
Wilhelm Reich Infant Trust

Renauld, Mary

The Persian Boy
New York: Bantam Books, 1972

Rosenbaum, Julius

The Plague of Lust
New York: Frederick Publications, 1955

Rossman, Parker

Sexual Experiences between Men and Boys
New York, 1976

Rothschild & Wolf

Children of the Counterculture
New York: Garden City, 1976

Rush, Florence

The Best Kept Secret
Sexual Abuse of Children
New Jersey: Prentice Hall, 1980

Sandfort, Theo

The Sexual Aspect of Pedophile Relations
The Experience of Twenty-five Boys
Amsterdam: Pan/Spartacus, 1982

BIBLIOGRAPHY

SATINOVER, JEFFREY

HOMOSEXUALITY AND THE POLITICS OF TRUTH
New York: Baker Books, 1996

SCARRO, A.M., JR. (ED.)

MALE RAPE
New York: Ams Press, 1982

SINGER, JUNE

ANDROGYNY
New York: Doubleday Dell, 1976

STEKEL, WILHELM

AUTO-EROTICISM
A Psychiatric Study of Onanism and Neurosis
Republished, London: Paul Kegan, 2004

PATTERNS OF PSYCHOSEXUAL INFANTILISM
New York, 1959 (reprint edition)

SADISM AND MASOCHISM
New York: W.W. Norton & Co., 1953

SEX AND DREAMS
The Language of Dreams
Republished
New York: University Press of the Pacific, 2003

SYMONDS, JOHN ADDINGTON

A PROBLEM IN GREEK ETHICS
New York: M.S.G. House, 1971

Vanguard, Thorkil

Phallós
A Symbol and its History in the Male World
New York: International Universities Press, 2001

Von Riezler, Sigmund

Geschichte der Hexenprozesse in Bayern
Stuttgart: Magnus Verlag, 1983

Ward, Elizabeth

Father-Daughter Rape
New York: Grove Press, 1985.

Yates, Alayne

Sex Without Shame: Encouraging the Child's Healthy Sexual Development
New York, 1978
Republished Internet Edition

Zukav, Gary

The Dancing Wu Li Masters
An Overview of the New Physics
New York: HarperOne, 2001

Personal Notes

www.ingramcontent.com/pod-product-compliance
Lightning Source LLC
Chambersburg PA
CBHW020451220526
45464CB00002B/952